IMAGES
of America

DELAWARE
ARMY NATIONAL GUARD

The Delaware Army National Guard organizational crest consists of a wreath, or twist of fabric of white and red, showing the guard's origin as an English colonial militia. Upon the wreath is a blue griffin's head, "torn" at the neck, representing the separation of Delaware from Pennsylvania in 1701. Its horns and beak are gold and its tongue is red. The collar is black, edged in silver or white, and upon the collar are three silver or white discs. The griffin is the principle device on the shield of the Lords de la Warr, for whom Delaware is named. The collar is from the shield of the Penn family, who were colonial governors. The griffin is particularly appropriate as a heraldic symbol because it symbolizes soldierly valor and a willingness to dare danger.

On the Cover: The noncommissioned officers of Company H, New Castle, pose at the Delaware Camp of 1913. Pictured from left to right are (first row) J. McCaugham, Irv Kirk, S. B. I. Duncan, Ed Naylor, unidentified, Jess McKay; (second row) Frank Harrington, unidentified, William E. Gell, Genford, unidentified, Wipf, and unidentified.

IMAGES
of America

DELAWARE ARMY NATIONAL GUARD

Brig. Gen. Kennard R. Wiggins Jr. (DE ANG Retired)

ARCADIA
PUBLISHING

ISBN 978-0-7385-6693-1

Published by Arcadia Publishing
Charleston, South Carolina

Printed in the United States of America

Library of Congress Control Number: 2009935500

For all general information contact Arcadia Publishing at:
Telephone 843-853-2070
Fax 843-853-0044
E-mail sales@arcadiapublishing.com
For customer service and orders:
Toll-Free 1-888-313-2665

Visit us on the Internet at www.arcadiapublishing.com

This book is dedicated to the gallant men and women of the Delaware National Guard, their loving families, supportive employers, and loyal friends.

Contents

ACKNOWLEDGMENTS

This project was a natural progression from an earlier work on the Delaware Air National Guard and serves as a companion piece, in what for me is a two-part whole. Maj. Gen. Frank Vavala encouraged me to write this book, and I have enjoyed his unwavering confidence and support in this endeavor. It is a book about the organization he leads and is an appreciation shared with several thousand all-volunteer members, or former members, their families, friends, and neighbors. Many more than I can count, or find room to name here, have demonstrated their dedication by adding bits to the history of the Delaware Guard. They have offered their stories, their photographs, and their very personal experiences over a period of decades to accumulate this history.

I would like to acknowledge the expert assistance of Donn Devine, who is the dean of Delaware National Guard historians. Everything here rests upon his broad intellectual shoulders. Thanks to William Duncan for his contributions, counsel, and assistance and to Connie Cooper of the Delaware Historical Society, who was very helpful in making material available to me. My gratitude to Jan Churchill for her editing expertise and to Glenn Watson, who taught an "upstater" the richness of "downstate" history. To Kirsten Fitzgerald and Sherrill Hughes for administrative support, and gratitude also to Jim Testerman, Jim Sulpezi, Ron Stewart, Vincent Orlando, William Smith, Wiley Blevins, Terry Wiley, Brendan Mackie, Eric Roberson, and countless other Delaware Guard members and retirees who were primary sources of information in identifying the historic images, especially the folks in the Delaware National Guard Retired Officers Association.

I am grateful to the Delaware Military Heritage and Education Foundation for providing access to its historic archival material and supporting this project. Unless otherwise noted, all the images in this book are courtesy of the Delaware Military Heritage and Education Foundation. Finally, I am indebted to my patient wife, Liz, and my family for their loving encouragement and support.

INTRODUCTION

In the United States, the National Guard has origins that go very deep in history. A European concept of a citizen army can be traced to Greek history and was carried on in various forms during the Roman Empire and Western culture to follow. The modern militia concept had vigorous roots in English history that were transplanted to the New World. A militia is a body of citizens temporarily organized to defend themselves, sometimes called a trainband. They are ordinarily volunteers, and they serve in their own community for the common defense. They are part-time soldiers and full-time citizens with families, jobs, and homes. This description is still largely true after three and a half centuries.

One of the first orders of business for the Virginia colony in 1607 was to fortify and defend itself against the indigenous natives. In 1620, the Massachusetts Bay Colony formed a militia for the same purpose. In Delaware, a Swedish colony was founded just two years later in 1638. The Swedish-Delaware colony militia was called out on August 31, 1655, to defend against a Dutch force at Fort Christina. The Dutch prevailed, and they gave the militia a peacetime structure that endured until the English took over. The presence of this militia helped to insure Delaware's independence as a separate colony of the three lower counties of Pennsylvania.

There were two militias in colonial times. The common or enrolled militia included all men between the ages of 18 and 45 and represented a manpower resource pool from which to draw. It is still roughly the basis upon which the selective service can draw in an emergency.

The volunteer militia was a subset of the enrolled militia. It was comprised of volunteers who trained regularly and served outside their home colony, and they usually had better firearms. It is this volunteer militia that carried Delaware's colors in the five colonial wars against the French, Spanish, and Native Americans—King William's War, Queen Anne's War, King George's War, the War of Jenkins' Ear, and the French and Indian War.

In the War of Independence, the Delaware militia distinguished itself out of proportion to its size. Col. John Haslet formed the Delaware Regiment of the Continental Army in January 1776. The regiment saw its first action at the Battle of Long Island in August of the same year. Fresh from its training camp, the regiment established a reputation for all future members to uphold by its magnificent conduct in the face of a British force that outnumbered them 10 to 1. With the Maryland Continentals, it maintained its lines for four hours in the face of withering artillery fire and then threw back an assault of eight battle-hardened British regiments, including the crack Black Watch. When the command finally came to withdraw, it retired in good order with its colors and prisoners through a supposedly impassable swamp back to the American defenses, where it was commended by George Washington.

Its further service in the Revolution reads like a roll call of important battles—White Plains, Trenton, Brandywine, Germantown, Paulus Hook, and Monmouth in the northern theater and then south for the battles of Camden, Cowpens, Hobkirk's Hill, 96 and Eutaw Springs, Guilford Courthouse, and represented by a recruit detachment, the siege of Yorktown. The regiment's losses at Camden were so heavy that it was reorganized as a single company under Robert Kirkwood, one of the outstanding small-unit leaders of the war, and attached to a Maryland regiment formed from the remnants of two brigades. Col. "Light Horse Harry" Lee summed up the Delaware Regiment's almost eight years of continuous fighting in a single sentence, "No regiment in the army surpassed it in soldiership."

Following the Revolution, the regimental traditions were continued through separate companies of volunteers attached to organizations of the common militia. All the volunteer companies saw service in the War of 1812, where they played an important part in driving off a British naval squadron that sought to control the vital Delaware River.

Capt. Donn Devine in his booklet, "The Delaware National Guard, A Historical Sketch," notes that in the Mexican War, though the government would not accept volunteer companies as such from Delaware, the Delaware Guardsmen were not content to stay at home. After much red tape, a statewide composite unit was finally accepted as a company in a new regular army regiment, the 11th Infantry, and went off to Mexico with it. After some action around Vera Cruz, the regiment went on to the Battles of Contreras, Churubusco, Molino del Rey, and Chapultepec, where the 11th's losses were so heavy it won the name "Bloody 11th." The Delaware unit did not escape this fate; only a handful of men returned. Chapultepec was immortalized in the Marine Corps hymn, "From the halls of Montezuma," but there were almost twice as many Delaware volunteers (80) there as U.S. Marines (46).

Despite their losses in the Mexican Campaign, the volunteer spirit did not die out. As the Civil War began in 1860, five companies had been reorganized. The following spring they once more were organized into a regiment and entered federal service as the 1st Delaware Infantry Volunteers. Eleven streamers on the regimental colors tell the tale of their four years in the Civil War—Peninsula, Antietam, Fredericksburg, Chancellorsville, Gettysburg, Virginia 1863, Wilderness, Spotsylvania, Cold Harbor, Petersburg, and Appomattox. At Gettysburg, as part of the II Corps near the "Bloody Angle," they went into battle under a colonel and came out under a first lieutenant so heavy were their losses.

In the Spanish-American War, the regiment volunteered as soon as war was declared, but much to the disappointment of the men, they failed to see action in that war—for the first time in the outfit's 122-year history. It is here that the photographic history in this book begins.

With the rest of the National Guard, the 1st Delaware went to New Mexico in 1916, where it received the seasoning that was to pay off in World War I. It was instrumental in developing the army truck as a useful weapon of war during the campaign. Only a month after its return, it was in service again. Converted to a new type of organization soon after, it saw service in France as the 59th Pioneer Infantry Regiment. The Meuse-Argonne streamer on the colors reminds veterans of the regiment of the harrowing days in the Argonne when they were laying railroad track and building water purification plants while under shell fire from the enemy.

After World War I, the regiment became an anti-aircraft outfit, the 198th Coast Artillery Regiment. One battalion was converted to coast defense, the 261st Coast Artillery Battalion (Harbor Defense). Both were called to duty in 1940. The 198th, which had twice won the Coast Artillery Association trophy as the top National Guard anti-aircraft (AA) outfit in the country, went to the South Pacific, where it served in the Northern Solomon's and Luzon Campaigns. It was awarded an arrowhead device on its Northern Solomon's streamer for the assault landing on Mono Island in the Treasuries and the Philippine Presidential Unit Citation for Luzon. The 261st did not go overseas as a unit, but after some months in the Harbor Defenses of the Delaware, it was broken up into cadres for new field artillery units for the European theater, where most of its members finally reached combat.

After the war, the Delaware Guard began reorganizing in June 1946 with the 198th Anti-Aircraft Artillery (AAA) group headquarters and the 736th and 945th AAA Battalions. It added an air unit in September 1946, the 142nd Fighter Squadron, which soon after came under the umbrella of the Air Force (see *Delaware Air National Guard*, a separate Arcadia publication). In 1949, the

Delaware Guard expanded to brigade strength adding HQ 261st AAA Brigade, the 160th AAA group, and two battalions.

The reorganization was underway when the Korean War erupted. The 736th AAA Battalion and several smaller units were called to federal service, which accounted for about one-third of the Delaware Army National Guard that reported for active duty.

Throughout the Cold War, much reorganization, expansion, and consolidation occurred in guard units, especially in Delaware. Initially two new anti-aircraft battalions, the 197th in Smyrna and the 945th in Laurel, were formed in the mid-1950s to meet these new challenges. In addition, two of Delaware's six battalions received the new self-propelled twin 40-mm "Dusters," and two other battalions received the 75-mm "Skysweeper" guns. At this time, the 116th Mobile Army Surgical Hospital was organized in Wilmington.

Then, in 1959, a major reorganization, based on the "Pentomic" division structure and the introduction of the Combat Arms Regimental System, took place within the guard. Under this reorganization, all of Delaware's artillery units once again became part of the old regiment, and the 198th Artillery (1st Delaware) became the regimental headquarters. The 156th Anti-Aircraft Battalion was re-designated as the 1st Battalion, 198th Artillery. Its headquarters battery, which dates back to the Revolutionary War, is the senior unit in the state.

The 1959 reorganization increased the need for combat service support troops, causing the 197th AAA Battalion to reorganize as the 109th Ordnance Battalion with a transportation helicopter maintenance company.

The Delaware Guard continued to fulfill state missions despite increasing Cold War demands. In March 1962, after a damaging nor'easter battered the area, over 2,000 Guardsmen were called upon for rescue, security, and recovery operations in the devastated coastal areas of Kent and Sussex Counties. In addition, the DEARNG's Dusters were used to get through several severe snowstorms during that time period.

Then, in 1962, the Army National Guard's five air defense outfits were again reorganized, this time into automatic weapon battalions. From this point on, the National Guard furnished not only all air defenses for army divisions, but also the automatic weapon capabilities.

Although not called to active duty for the Vietnam War, Delaware Army Guard members fulfilled vital roles that made possible the heavy commitment of active forces there. From the start of the buildup in Vietnam, numbers of individual Delaware Guard members, especially aviators, volunteered for active duty.

The first unit contribution came in the fall of 1964, when the army was testing the concept of the Airmobile Division in response to requirements from Vietnam. Since the army had no active Duster units, Delaware's 2nd Battalion, 198th Artillery, was called on to support the U.S. Army's 82nd Airborne Division in a full-scale field test of the concept. Successful results of the test led to the almost immediate organization of the 1st Cavalry Division (Airmobile) and its deployment to Vietnam.

Early in 1966, a number of Army National Guard enlisted specialists volunteered for six months service as instructors at Fort Bliss, Texas, when the army found it lacked men capable of training new personnel about the intricacies of the M-42 Duster. In this select force were seven Delaware units—the five batteries of the 1st Battalion, 198th Artillery—comprising about one-third of the Delaware Army Guard strength. Other Delaware units contributed to their readiness by furnishing fully trained replacements to the Selected Reserve Force units when necessary.

Following the assassination of Rev. Martin Luther King Jr. in 1967, riots broke out in 19 major American cities. Some 68,000 National Guardsmen and 22,600 U.S. Army troops were called upon to suppress the outbreaks. In its first large-scale state activation, on April 9, 1968, the Delaware National Guard was called to state duty to quell civil disturbances and violence in the city of Wilmington, Delaware. The unit was released from state duty after several weeks. However, many individuals remained on state duty through January 20, 1969.

With the end of conscription and the onset of the all-volunteer force, Delaware faced recruiting and retention challenges shared by the rest of America's military as it downsized and licked its wounds over the Vietnam War and the rebuilding years to follow. For the first time, Delaware hired and employed full-time recruiters and later offered enlistment bonuses. The all-volunteer force was implemented in January 1973 by Secretary of Defense Laird, who terminated induction of draftees. It forced two major social transformations on the National Guard. First, it became a racially integrated organization because of pressure to admit blacks and the need to secure additional manpower. Second, it included women on a significant scale for the first time.

In November 1990, the 249th Engineer Detachment and the 736th Supply and Service Battalion of the Delaware Army National Guard were placed on alert status and very shortly thereafter placed on active duty to participate in Operation Desert Shield.

The 249th was a 70-person unit consisting of carpenters, electricians, brick masons, plumbers, and pipe fitters whose mission was to provide facilities engineering at fixed installations. Their mission in Saudi Arabia was to maintain a military base camp with the number of personnel reaching 25,000. They built and repaired facilities along with minor road and construction work. After the war, the 249th completely overhauled an abandoned recreation center. Thousands of soldiers were able to reap the benefits of the 249th's efforts in the center.

The 736th had over 60 personnel who provided services to troops in the field. They distributed supplies and food, controlled critical inventory, and managed logistics for King Khalid Military City. This included operating Log Base Bravo, post exchanges, mess halls, and the clothing facility.

The war in Afghanistan commenced on October 7, 2001, with the purpose of eliminating Al-Qaeda terrorist training camps, as well as securing the capture of Osama bin Laden.

The Iraq War began on March 20, 2003, with the U.S. and U.K.–led invasion against Saddam Hussein's terror-based regime. Since then, the Delaware National Guard (DNG) has vigilantly supported Operation Iraqi Freedom. Soldiers and airmen from all across the state answered their country's call once again.

Delaware army and air units and individuals have supported Operation Iraqi Freedom since 2003. The first of these units to arrive in Baghdad was the 249th Engineer Detachment. The 249th was federally mobilized from February 2003 until April 2004. The detachment supported reconstruction efforts throughout the capital city, Baghdad, Iraq.

The Delaware Army National Guard makes a contribution to the defense of the United States on a continuing basis.

Glossary

AAA—Anti-Aircraft
AAA—Anti-Aircraft Artillery
ADA—Air Defense Artillery
AW—Automatic Weapons
CWO—Chief Warrant Officer
DEARNG—Delaware Army National Guard
HHD—Headquarters Detachment
PFC—Private First Class
MSG—Master Sergeant
SFC—Sergeant First Class
SP—Self-Propelled
SPC—Specialist

One

A New Century

The photographic record of the Delaware militia prior to the Spanish-American War is very sparse, although two images from the Civil War era are included in this book.

In 1894, the general assembly designated the Delaware troops of the militia as the "National Guard of Delaware." At this time it was stronger as a social organization than as a disciplined military force. The Spanish-American War revealed these weaknesses once again. The encampments of 1889–1890 were held at Brandywine Springs.

The Dick Act of 1903 for the first time provided federal funds for training and later authorized guardsmen to serve overseas. In 1902, the Delaware National Guard consisted of one regiment of infantry, with seven companies, and a band with 28 officers commanding 322 men. A year before, the entire outfit participated in President McKinley's inauguration. A new company was formed in Newark; Company E after the Bridgeville unit was mustered out. In summer 1902, and again in 1904, they camped near historic Cooch's Bridge and indulged in drills, rifle practice, and social intercourse wearing their broad-brimmed campaign hats.

Two battalions were sent to Deming, New Mexico, in July 1916 for border patrol duties during the Pancho Villa border incursion incident. They were led by Maj. William E. Lank and Maj. J. Warner Reed. This deployment proved to be valuable experience for World War I.

Of the men who received their first military training in the ranks of the Delaware battalions, the most famous is Lt. Gen. John W. "Iron Mike" O'Daniel, who was a private and later supply sergeant in Newark's Company E. Among the officers were two later adjutants general of Delaware, J. A. Ellison and William Berl Jr., and a future commander of the Delaware regiment, John P. LeFevre.

By early 1917, the situation was well under control, and the guardsmen returned to their homes. Residents of Wilmington recalled the memorable "welcome home" banquet at the Hotel DuPont on February 7, 1917—the largest ever held up to that time in Wilmington.

This 1865 image depicts Brig. Gen. Thomas Smyth and staff at Headquarters 2nd Division, Second Army Corps at "Hatchens Run" in Virginia.

Lt. Abraham G. Wolf of the 1st Delaware Heavy Artillery at Fort Delaware (1863–1864) is seated center left; the other soldiers are from Battery G, Pittsburgh Heavy Artillery. (Courtesy Brendan Mackie collection.)

The 1st Delaware Infantry, in the Spanish-American War—1898, stands in formation.

In a tented camp, near Middletown, Delaware, named for Gov. Ebe W. Tunnell, men of the 1st Delaware Infantry relax during the Spanish-American War in 1898.

Four unnamed Delaware troopers pose with their weapons by their tent in Camp Tunnell near Middletown, Delaware, during the Spanish-American War in 1898.

Pictured is the 1st Delaware Infantry Regiment during the Spanish-American War. Note the African American man reclining in front (not in uniform).

The Delaware Rifle Team, captained by W. E. Lank, poses for the camera at Sea Girt, New Jersey, for the National Matches in 1903.

A postcard from the annual encampment at Rehoboth Beach, Delaware, July 31, 1908, reads, "Dear Mother, I am well, went on Guard Wednesday at 4 PM and came off Thursday at 4 PM feet a little sore a coon cut a soldiers head with a brick the soldiers chased 400 out of town pretty near killed three Good bye."

A color guard of the 1st Delaware Infantry stands for a parade in 1914.

The Delaware Rifle Team poses at a competition in Jacksonville, Florida, in 1916. Among them is 1st Sgt. Frederick L. Manion of Company F, one of the nation's outstanding marksmen, who brought added laurels to the Delaware National Guard that year by placing second in the National Matches with the high-powered rifle at Camp Perry, Ohio.

This postcard shows soldiers on the march from a train in Rehoboth, Delaware, on July 27, 1908. The back of the card states, "Camp Hall, Rehoboth arrived safe haven't had anything to eat from 6 this a.m. till 5 p.m. from working hard to."

Capt. Robert M. Carswell (later colonel, U.S. Army, 1st Delaware Infantry) poses in a desert landscape near Deming, New Mexico, in 1916.

Capt. J. Austin Ellison stands in a tented camp in Deming, New Mexico in 1916. He later served as Delaware adjutant general.

Robert Ferguson, of the 1st Delaware Infantry, poses during the Mexican Border Campaign in 1916.

Pictured here serving drinks at the bar are, from left to right, Ludwig, Waler Farren, Edwards, George Susa, Lemwell Johnson, two unidentified, Arnell, three unidentified, Joe Farren, Merideth, unidentified, Curtis, and Hayman Hall.

Maj. J. Warner Reed, commander of the 1st Delaware Infantry during the Mexican Border Incursion, is seated at tented quarters in Deming, New Mexico, in 1916.

Delaware officers and noncommissioned officers pose in camp with their Delaware sign. Maj. Warner Reed, commander of the 1st Delaware Infantry, is third from the left in the second row.

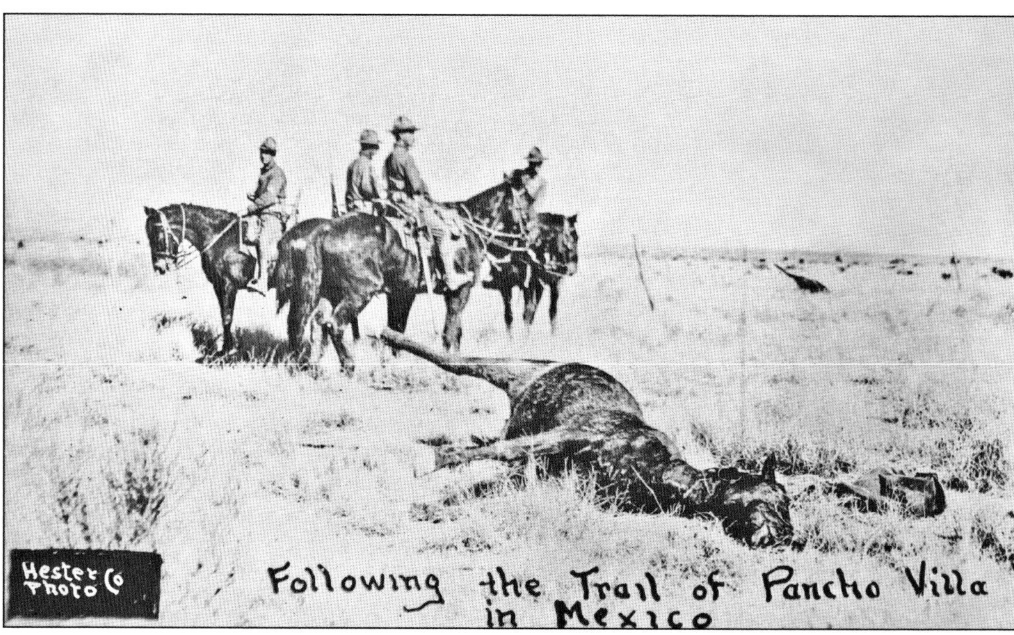

On this image, it is simply stated, "Following the trail of Pancho Villa in Mexico."

"Uncle Sam's new fighting machine on the border," depicts an armored truck. Delaware helped to develop the truck as a weapon. In 1911, the army owned only 12 trucks. By the end of 1916, there were 22 companies on the border with 25 trucks each.

Mexican cavalrymen display their shooting skills on horseback.

This photograph depicts soldiers of the Mexican Border Campaign in 1916. They are from the 1st Delaware Infantry. Pictured from left to right are (first row) Wilmer Chadwick, unidentified; (second row, kneeling) Robert Ferguson, John Pennington; (third row, standing) Dutch Ludwig, Len Johnson, John Sproul, and James J. Houghton.

George Rodney poses during the Mexican Border Campaign, 1916.

Two

The Great War

Released from service on the Mexican border in the spring of 1917, the 1st Delaware Regiment enjoyed only the briefest respite before being called to federal service once again in April 1917 as America declared war on Germany.

Some of the officers who were to lead the 198th Coast Artillery in World War II had just started the ascension through the enlisted ranks, including Brig. Gen. George J. Schulz and Lt. Cols. S. B. I. Duncan and Henry C. Ray. Delaware's future state director of selective service, Brig. Gen. Harry B. Van Sciver, was a second lieutenant in Company C.

Many individual recruits were scattered throughout the American Expeditionary Force, and only one unit can fairly be called a Delaware unit—the 59th Pioneer Infantry. Under the leadership of Col. J. Warren Reed, they assembled at the rifle range near New Castle until being moved to Camp McClellan, Alabama, in October 1917.

After further duties at Fort Dix, New Jersey, and a visit by Delaware governor Townsend, they embarked for France on the USS *Leviathan* in August 1918. They were assigned to the First Army Area. Companies A and F were engaged in road building and maintenance; Company B operated a concrete block factory; Companies E and H did general construction; Company G was a camouflage unit; Companies C, D, I, and M worked on water supply by building and operating reservoirs, treatment plants, and pipelines; and Companies K and L built and repaired railways.

The 3rd Battalion Companies I, K, L, and M did their work in the Argonne Forest at the height of the battle, building their water and railway systems under almost continuous air raids and shell fire, including gas shells. This is commemorated on the colors of the present-day Delaware National Guard descendants of the 59th—the 198th Signal Battalion—by a rainbow-hued battle streamer for Meuse-Argonne.

This postcard of Delaware troops is labeled, "Company A 114th at Company Front, Camp McClellan, Alabama."

Camp Townsend, 1st Delaware Regiment, at Camp Dix, New Jersey, in September 1917 is depicted here.

Alvan Morgan poses before an American flag on the eve of his deployment overseas.

This postcard is labeled, "Awkward squad, Mobilization Camp, Syracuse, New York." The card is postmarked August 1, 1918, and reads, "Everything going well. Tell the folks I was asking for them also my address is Recruit Camp, 3rd Company, 1st Battalion—Alvan. [Morgan]."

Col. J. Warner Reed, regimental commander of the 1st Delaware Infantry during World War I, is depicted in this period photograph.

This is 2nd Lt. Harry B. Van Sciver of Company C. Van Sciver would later serve as the Selective Service director for Delaware in the 1950s.

Lieutenant S. B. I. Duncan was later elected to command Battery H of New Castle. It is said that he was the last officer to be so elected.

Capt. J. Danforth Bush, seen here in France in 1919, was later to serve as the lieutenant governor of Delaware from 1921 until 1925.

The postcard obverse states, "Mangiennes, France, January 3, 1919, To Schulz—Handsome George with his blue black hair, favorite topic, 'Some lady fair,' Morn, noon, or night, nor miss a meal rare, Favorite duty, 'ducking his prayer.'—Jones."

Capt. Harry B. Smith poses on February 18, 1919, at Toul, France. According to Smith, "This crop is one month old." Smith would later retire as a lieutenant colonel.

Lt. George Schulz is depicted here. He was later destined to lead the 198th Coast Artillery in World War II.

Capt. Charles R. Jeffries Jr. is shown here in LeMans, France, on June 9, 1919, with the 59th Pioneer Infantry Regiment.

Chaplain Howard Davis of the 1st Delaware Infantry sits for the camera.

Capt. James L. Scotton of the 1st Delaware Infantry is depicted in his uniform.

Capt. Lewis J. Ellison, of the 59th Pioneer Infantry, poses in France, 1918.

Maj. Jesse A. McKay of the 59th Pioneer Infantry is depicted here.

This photograph is labeled, "Les Marechaux francais et allies a Metzm," which translates to "The French Field Marshalls and their allies." Pictured in front from left to right are Joseph Joffre, Ferdinand Foch, Douglas Haig, John "Black Jack" Pershing, and Phillipe H. Petain.

A presentation photograph of the 59th Pioneer Infantry Band at Monte Carlo in 1919 is "presented by Capt. D. M. Salter, C.O.Hq. Co. 59th Pioneer Inf. to H. B. Van Sciver." Note the swastika motif on the bass drum in the center. It was an Indian symbol for good luck and was used as the Delaware symbol from the Civil War to the early 1930s.

This is a postbellum group picture at a party given by Governor Miller for officers of the 59th Pioneer Infantry.

This image depicts Capt. D. M. Salter of the 1st Delaware Infantry.

Maj. Alfred S. Hirzel stands for the camera at Le Mans, France, on June 10, 1919.

Lt. Horace Wilkinson poses at Camp Dix, New Jersey.

Three

Between the Wars

At the conclusion of the Great War, the 59th Pioneer Infantry was assigned to pick up munitions and supplies left by the Germans after the armistice was signed. Arriving home in the spring of 1919, the 59th disembarked at Hoboken, New Jersey. About 9,191 men from Delaware served in World War I and about 2,000 of them were with the 59th Pioneer Infantry.

This left the state without a military organization. The National Guard Bureau allotted Delaware one battalion of infantry and two companies of coast artillery. By 1921, the 198th Coast Artillery (anti-aircraft) had a complement of 38 officers and 717 enlisted men. The 261st Coast Artillery was formed in 1924 with Battery A at Laurel with three officers and 65 enlisted men. In 1936, Battery B was activated at Georgetown and Batter C of Dover followed in 1940.

In 1928, the Delaware National Guard opened its military reservation at Bethany Beach. The organization began the peacetime routine of regular summer encampments and drills as they attempted to rebuild and train. The 198th Coast Artillery twice won the Coast Artillery Association trophy as the top National Guard outfit in the country during this period.

By 1940, strength had increased to 1,369, including 501 new recruits following the declaration of emergency by President Roosevelt in September 1939. The National Guard Bureau had authorized a 69-percent increase so the personnel on the eve of World War II would be 1,800 men in the 198th Coast Artillery and 876 in the 261st Coast Artillery and a total of 2,698 statewide. Both units were called to active service by President Roosevelt prior to Pearl Harbor in September 1940.

At the end of the summer 1941, the 198th moved to Fort Ontario, New York, and 36 hours after Pearl Harbor, they had packed and loaded equipment, drawn ammunition, made a motor march of 300 miles on icy roads, and set up tactical positions to defend the Pratt and Whitney aircraft factory at East Hartford, Connecticut. It was a remarkable feat and a tribute to the regiment's training.

A parade of veterans marches in 1922 on the Washington Street Bridge over the Brandywine River in Wilmington, Delaware.

In this photograph, Delaware participants in the marksmanship National Matches pose in 1920. (Courtesy the Charles Arnold collection.)

This 1923 postcard from Camp Hamilton, New York, is labeled, "Camp Upton JB then a Sgt." (Courtesy the Charles Arnold collection.)

Soldiers score their marksmanship training targets at River Road, New Castle, Delaware, in 1929.

Many future Delaware National Guard leaders are depicted here at summer camp in Bethany Beach. Pictured from left to right are Stark, Hudgeons, Le Feore, Lotz, Schulz, Townsend, Van Sciver, Sipple, Dugan, Clark, Barsky, Scottone, and Wiekiuem.

A target-towing airplane serves as the backdrop during annual training at the Bethany Beach military reservation in the 1930s. In this photograph from left to right are the adjutant general, George Schulz, S. B. I. Duncan, and Harry Van Sciver.

Trophies from 1930 are depicted in this group photograph. Pictured are, from left to right, Schulz, Ellison, Lefevre, Lank, Huntington, Townsend, Hastings, Birch, and Houston.

Alvin Roberson demonstrates the tripod-mounted, water-cooled .30-caliber machine gun in the 1930s at Bethany Beach, Delaware. (Courtesy Eric Roberson collection.)

The Delaware National Guard baseball team poses with George Schulz (in the second row wearing a derby).

Officers pose in 1935. Pictured from left to right are (first row) Hudson, Davis, Rosco, Schultz, Grier, and Ashton; (second row) among the men are Apostolico, Holt, Stevens, Majewski, and Harrington.

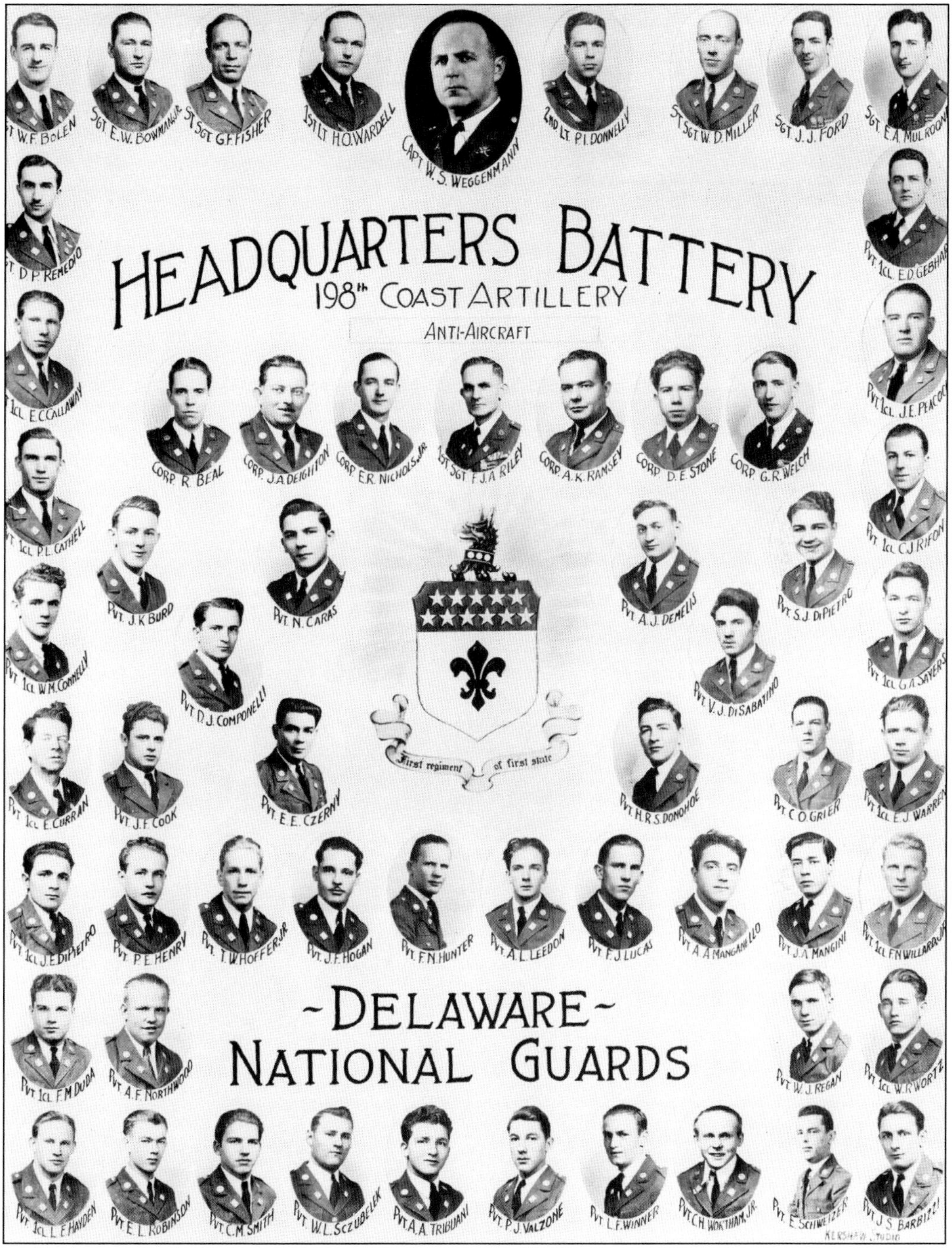

This presentation poster depicts the Headquarters Battery, 198th Coast Artillery Anti-Aircraft.

A Delaware National Guard machine-gun crew stands in an informal pose during the 1930s.

Cookie and his crew stand outside a hot kitchen during the annual summer camp.

This image depicts Brig. Gen. Weller E. Stover, the adjutant general of Delaware from 1931 to 1940.

Two soldiers are depicted on "Kitchen Patrol" with the soldier on the left peeling potatoes and the soldier on the right studying the "New Castle-Pennsville Ferry Schedule." A note on the obverse states, "Paint the time-table white so it looks like a letter from home."

Pictured here are an anti-aircraft gun and its crew practicing at Camp Upton in Long Island, New York.

The 1940 Camp Upton staff is depicted before their tents. Pictured from left to right are (first row) Schulz, Duncan, and Barsky; (second row) Kushner and the rest are unidentified.

This is an example of a Saturday morning inspection held in the barracks at Camp Upton in Long Island, New York.

The troops "fall in" for inspection at a tented camp.

This image shows preliminary marksmanship training, using M1903 rifles, that was conducted at Camp Upton.

The 198th was called up for federal service on September 16, 1940, by Presidential Executive Order No. 8530 for one year. The greatest peacetime mobilization in the nation's history was getting under way with National Guardsmen in hundreds of units in 27 different states answering the first call to the colors. By mid-1941, months before Pearl Harbor, the entire National Guard would be on active duty—nearly all would serve for five years or more.

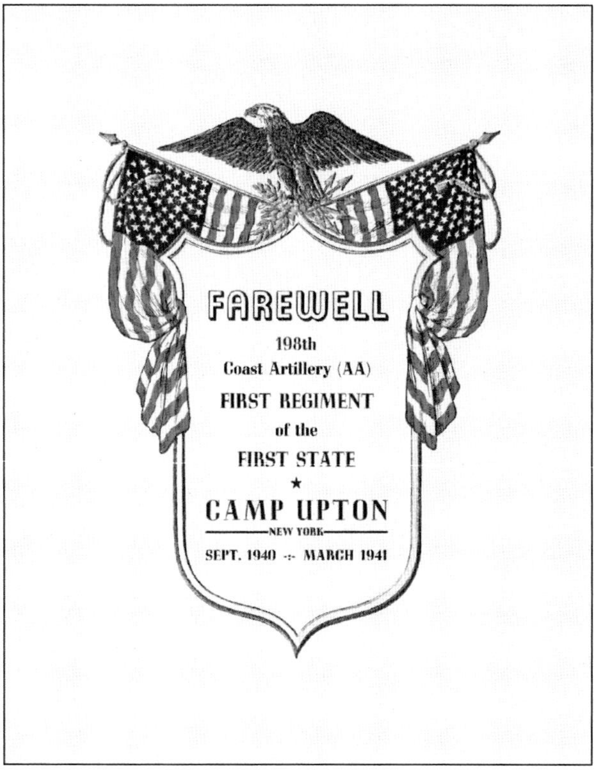

A parade reviewing party is depicted here. Pictured are, from left to right, unidentified, Barsky, Huntington, two unidentified, Kushner, Schulz, and two unidentified.

A farewell program is shown here, and the inscription inside states, "The Officers and men of the 198th Coast Artillery (AA) leave Camp Upton for their new station with the respect and best wishes of the Officers of my command. You are indeed The First Regiment of the First State. C. W. Baird, Commanding."

Four

World War II

After Pearl Harbor, word came that the regiment was to move overseas, and on January 16, 1942, it left for Charleston, South Carolina, the port of embarkation. The 198th was the first U.S. unit to leave for overseas after the outbreak of war—another tribute to its superb training and the high regard in which it was held.

The first station overseas was greeted with delight. It was the island of Bora Bora, known for security purposes as "Bobcat Island." The regiment spent a year there fortifying the island against the probability that the Japanese drive might not be slowed down before they reached the Society Islands.

In January 1943, the 198th moved to Efate, in the New Hebrides, and in October to Guadalcanal. The regiment as a unit came to an end in February 1944 when it was reorganized. Most of the original Delaware members of the regiment had returned to the United States to attend Officer Candidate School (OCS), to train replacements, or to organize new units. More than one-quarter of the regiment's enlisted men won commissions.

Delaware's 261st Coast Artillery Battalion was a harbor defense unit charged with defending the Delaware Bay. Shortly after entering federal service, it went into "temporary" bivouac on the sand dunes at Cape Henlopen.

Before the battalion was through, the bivouac had become the $20-million Fort Miles, the most modern and best equipped coast defense installation on the Atlantic Coast, and the 261st played a major part in setting up and manning the fort. As a unit, the 261st did not see action in World War II, but by late 1943, most of the original members had been transferred out to serve as cadre personnel for the many new field artillery units being trained for the invasion of Europe. Almost all of the men of the 261st saw overseas service as individuals before the war was over.

In this photograph are (left) Capt. A. W. Adams and Maj. Ralph S. Baker at Camp Henlopen in Lewes, Delaware, in December 1941. The tent was used as officer's quarters from the establishment of Camp Henlopen until permanent buildings were completed and it was renamed Fort Miles in 1942. Hot water for showers was provided by the sun on pipes running across the sand.

Company A of Delaware State Guard poses before the Wilmington Armory. Pictured in the front center are Capt. Walter M. Deputy (right) and Adj. Lt. Thomas C. Sullivan (left). The Delaware State Guard assumed "home guard" duties as the 198th deployed overseas, filling the gap left by the deploying guardsmen.

Col. George Schulz, of Hartley, Delaware, the commander of the 198th Coast Artillery during World War II, was a veteran of the Mexican Campaign and World War I.

The regimental staff is shown at Bobcat Island, Bora Bora, in late July 1942. Pictured from left to right are (first row) Cook, Barsky, Schulz, Huntington, and Holt; (second row) Peterson, Weatherby, Riker, Kushner, Orth, and Wilson.

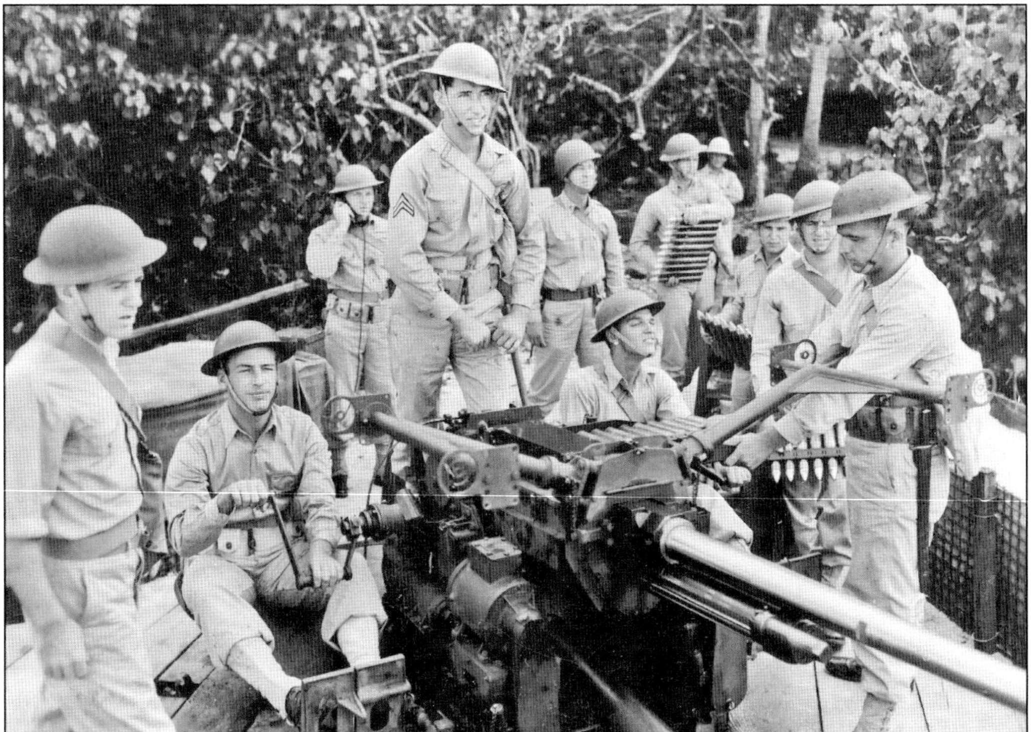
A gun emplacement manned by soldiers of the 198th on Bora Bora readies for action.

A bunker is shown on Bobcat Island, the classified name for Bora Bora.

A gas-attack drill is being conducted by soldiers in a jungle clearing.

Typical field conditions of a jungle motor pool are depicted here.

An improvised lift for truck maintenance demonstrates the ingenuity of the "grease monkeys" of the 198th.

A moment of relaxation for sunning soldiers among the tropical fronds is depicted in this photograph.

Soldiers of the 198th are ready for action, outfitted and posing in a state of preparedness before their quarters.

Communications were critical. These soldiers make expedient use of a palm tree as a telephone pole.

Wires are strung to link the compound for communication, command, and control.

An operator at the switchboard of the communications shack is shown here.

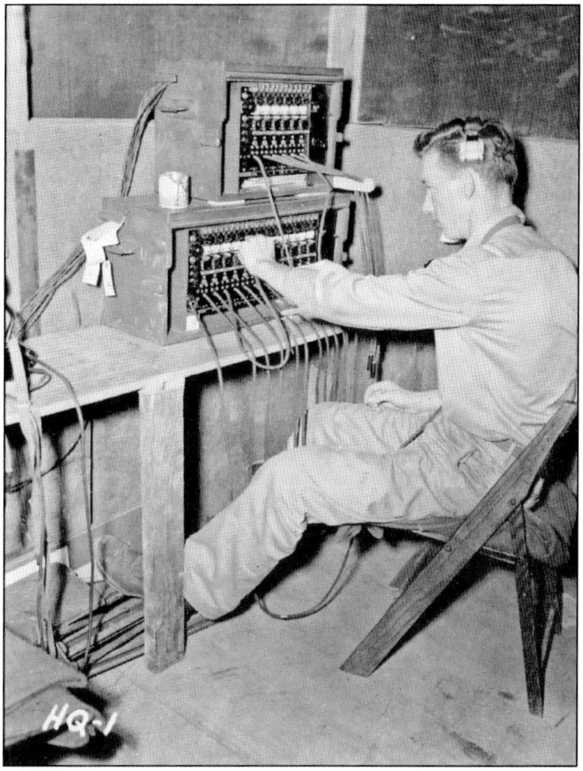

An apt description of this photograph might be, "Praise the Lord, and pass the .30-caliber armor-piercing ammunition."

A stage show known as the "Bobcat Follies" was held at Bora Bora to raise morale. From the diary of Lt. Col. David Harrington on February 22, 1942, "The natives put on a hula-hula dance at 2000. The governor came over from Tahiti."

Seven unidentified soldiers from the 198th Coast Artillery at Bora Bora are shown here. In January 1943, the 198th moved to Efate, in the New Hebrides, where it again prepared defensive positions.

The band played an essential role in maintaining morale and providing entertainment for the deployed troops.

An anti-aircraft artillery crew in a sandbagged gun pit trains their weapon for enemy aircraft. In October 1943, the unit prepared to go into action against the enemy and moved to Guadalcanal. There it became the only army unit assigned to the Marine 1st Amphibious Corps, and it participated in the assault landing on Mono Island in the Treasury Group on October 25th.

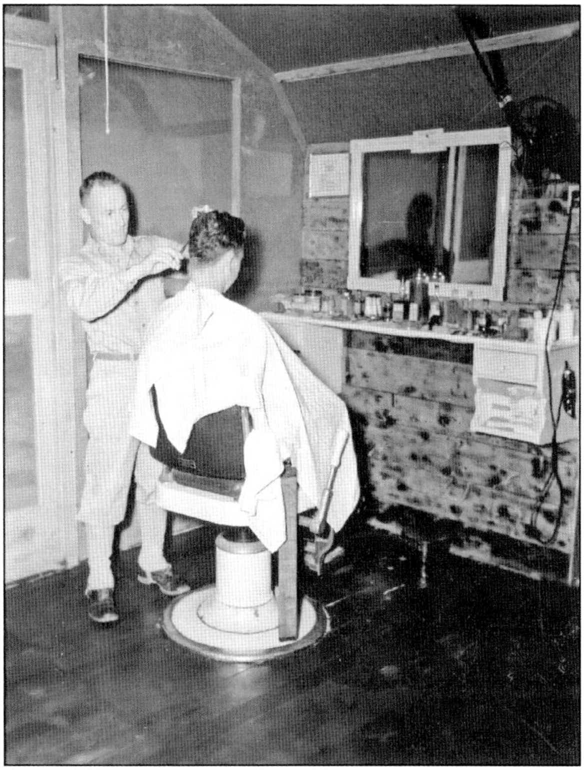

Even in a war zone, essential services such as barbering were established in the Quonset huts.

Searchlights were used by the unit to seek enemy aircraft in the night skies for anti-aircraft artillery targeting.

Worship services were held alfresco under tropical palms on Bora Bora.

GIs man the guns at Bobcat Island. From the diary of Lt. Col. David Harrington on May 24, 1942, "Test fired the 37 mm guns of Battery 'H,' 198th C. A. today. Everything OK." Pictured is a 90-mm gun crew.

In this photograph, Lt. Col. Joseph M. Barsky (left), the regimental surgeon, departs Bora Bora for the United States in 1942 as Lt. Col. H. Wallace Cooke (with glasses) and Col. George Schulz (shaking hands with Barsky) bid farewell.

Five

After the War

By the time World War II ended, all state enlistments in the National Guard had expired. The difficult task of reorganizing began in June 1946, and 15 months later, the National Guard had fully organized the 198th AAA Group Headquarters and the 736th and 945th AAA Battalions. In 1946, the Delaware Air Guard was organized as the 142nd Fighter Squadron and was a separate state service.

In 1949, the Delaware Army Guard was authorized to expand to brigade strength. In June 1950, North Korea moved south across the 38th Parallel and the United States was at war again. The 736th AAA Battalion was at summer camp when word came of its order into federal service. About one-third of the Delaware Army National Guard went on active duty.

The 736th served at Fort Meade, Maryland, where with its 90-mm guns it became one of the first units in the newly established Air Defense of Baltimore and Washington, D.C. By the time the unit was returned to the state in 1952, few of its original members were still with it. Most had been transferred, and many saw combat service in Korea with other units under the policy of individual replacement then in effect.

Throughout the Cold War much reorganization, expansion, and consolidation occurred in National Guard units, especially in Delaware. Initially two new anti-aircraft battalions, the 197th in Smyrna and the 945th in Laurel, were formed in the mid-1950s to meet these new challenges. In addition, two of Delaware's six battalions received the new self-propelled twin 40-mm "Dusters," and two other battalions received the 75-mm "Skysweeper" guns. At this time, the 116th Mobile Army Surgical Hospital was organized in Wilmington.

Then in 1959, a major reorganization, based on the "Pentomic" division structure, took place within the National Guard. All of Delaware's artillery units once again became part of the old regiment, and the 198th Artillery (1st Delaware) became the regimental headquarters. The 156th Anti-Aircraft Battalion was re-designated as 1st Battalion, 198th Artillery. Its headquarters battery, which dated back to the Revolutionary War, is the senior unit in the state.

A June 1950 formal portrait of Brig. Gen. Joseph J. Scannell, adjutant general of Delaware, is shown here.

The Milford Armory is the setting for three Delaware soldiers.

An honor guard is depicted at Bethany Beach, on July 28, 1950, at Headquarters Battery of the 736th AAA Gun Battalion. Pictured here are, from left to right, (first row) Arthurs, Walter Deputy Jr., Nisky, Raymond Deputy, J. O. Brown, Joseph T. Smith, D. Smith, Hugg, Sammons, Brower; (second row) Lt. Francis Marshall, Bennett, Sharpley, Kneckt, Roland Diefenderfer, Davis, Garman, Grant, Hamilton, DeMatteo, 1st Sgt. Walter Deputy, and Finney. (Joseph Smith collection.)

The "steno pool" busies itself at state headquarters in the Wilmington Armory during the Korean War in 1950. Pictured from left to right are Joseph "Sonny" Smith, typist Roland Diefenderfer, "Kid" Davis, and regular army instructor Arthur Brower. (Joseph Smith collection.)

The 736th AAA is shown here in 1952, with Lt. Col. Frank T. Lynch in the foreground and, from left to right, Capt. John Stopyra, Capt. Gregory Dillon, and Capt. Blair Zebley.

In August 1953, Brig. Gen. Scannell and Maj. Gen. L. D. Carter, commanding general of the Second Army, inspect a 90-mm anti-aircraft gun at South Bethany Range. It is being manned by Sgt. John Sullivan of Battery C of the 736th AAA Gun Battalion.

In a photograph depicting the end of federal service in 1952, the 736th AAA Battalion is shown here. Pictured from left to right are (first row) unidentified, General Scannell, General Moore, Colonel Grier, and two unidentified; (second row) Col. F. T. Lynch on the far left and the rest are unidentified.

In November 1953, the annual track and field meets were held at Bethany Beach. Presentation of the winning team trophy by Brig. Gen. Joseph J. Scannell to Capt. (Chaplain) Francis J. Tierney, who is accepting for the 156th AAA Gun Battalion, is depicted. To the left of General Scannell are Col. Edwin Thompson (second to left), commissioned officer of 156th AAA Group of the Virginia National Guard, and Lt. Col. Preston Lee (far left), commissioned officer of the 156th AAA Gun Battalion of the Delaware National Guard.

The Delaware National Guard State Staff poses in 1955. Pictured from left to right are (first row) Raymond Holland, unidentified, Paul Desmond, George Fisher, Edward Vernon Hill, Donn Devine, and David Snellenberg; (second row) George Walton, George Sylvester, Walter H. Pyle, Joseph J. Scannell, Paul Donnelly, John Grier, D. Preston Lee, and Maxwell Reed.

The Governor's Ball in 1956 was held at the Allan Mclane Armory in Smyrna, Delaware.

The January 1956 reassignment of Company C, 736th as Company A, 156th is depicted here. Battery C, 736th AAA Battalion of Newark, Delaware, was reassigned as Battery A, 156th AAA Battalion. The battalion was commanded by Lt. Col. James G. Maloney. Battery A was commanded by Capt. Donald Paisley. Pictured here from left to right are unidentified, Lt. Col. James G. Maloney, Capt. Donald L. Paisley, 2nd Lt. Daniel J. Smith, and Master Sergeant John L. Sullivan.

Maj. Gen. John B. Moore, a veteran of the South Pacific with the 198th Coast Artillery, poses for his portrait.

A 60-mile fitness hike in 1959 included Army Guardsman Ron Salomon (front left), an unidentified U.S. Marine (front, second from left) and Air National Guardsman Lt. Max O. Beheler (front, second from right).

Miss Delaware is flanked by brass and dignitaries at the Armed Forces Day celebration.

Second Lt. Arthur Episcopo, communicates on a field telephone from Battery C, 1st Battalion, 198th Artillery.

The Wilmington Armory, with a Hawk missile battery display entitled "America's Power on Land," is depicted here in 1960.

A parade is conducted here before the front gate at the Bethany Beach training site. The reviewing officers on the far left are Herbert Wardell and D. Robinson.

Armed Forces Day parade spectators are awed by the soldiers in formation.

Spectators at the Armed Forces Day celebration are shown here in 1960.

Seen here in 1959, a formation of soldiers forms "N. G." for the National Guard.

A ceremony was held in March 1959 at the grave site of Gen. Thomas A. Smyth, a Delaware Civil War general and the last Union general to die in combat.

The "Blue Hen" Ceremonial Unit, First Delaware Regiment marches on parade at New Castle Airport on Armed Forces Day.

Members of the ceremonial unit "the American Rifles" stand guard on the steps of the Wilmington Armory in 1959. Pictured here are SPC 6 Emerson Godfrey (left) and Master Sergeant Charles DePrisco.

A parade formation passes in review on Armed Forces Day in 1960.

The S. B. I. Duncan Awards were conducted in 1966 at the Armed Forces Day event at New Castle Airport. Pictured in front from left to right are Capt. Carl T. Butterworth, unidentified recipient, Mrs. S. B. I. Duncan, Newell Duncan, and Lt. Col. William Duncan.

Armed Forces Day is celebrated by a crowd at the New Castle Airport in May 1961.

The 287th Army Band entertains at Rodney Square in Wilmington to celebrate "This is the Army 1960."

The 287th Army Band, Delaware Army National Guard, under the baton of CWO E. Russell Williams, performs at a Memorial Day ceremony at Delaware Park in 1962.

The 287th Army Band performs during the summer of 1961. Note the short pants.

287th Army Band practices in a warehouse storage facility at the Bethany Beach training site.

A military formation marches in Wilmington, Delaware, on Market Street during the annual Memorial Day Parade.

The governor's inaugural parade (Governor Terry) marches in Dover, Delaware, on January 19, 1965. In front in this photograph, from left to right, are D. Robinson, Layton Johnson, and Vernon Hill.

The caption on this photograph is labeled, "National Guard picks up 20 yards. Ronnie Burcham, carrier, Chuck Morris runs interference behind him." Both are members of the 156th AAA Gun Battalion of Wilmington.

Tom Otto points to the basket as teammate Mike McGough, in the white jersey, goes for a rebound against Tom Machulski of the 1049th Transportation Company. Otto and McGough both play for B Company, 1st Battalion.

The Delaware National Guard basketball team is depicted in 1967–1968. Pictured from left to right are (first row) Ronald Park, Dave Turgis, Mel Gershman, Max O. Beheler, and John Redmond; (second row) Frank Szczerba, Edward Hoffman, Pete Szczerba, Thomas Otto, William Rutherford, Richard Jennings, and William Reader.

The Delaware National Guard pistol team, at Camp Perry, Ohio, is shown in 1965. As stated on the back of the image, pictured from left to right are Lt. Col. Carl L. Dawson, HHD 109 Ordnance Bn (Ammo), Major Russell G. Doyle, 166 USAF Dispensary, (second row) Lt. Col. George R. Walton, state HHD, Maj. Michael F. Riley Jr. state HHD, Lt. Col. William L. Deneke Hq Del ANG, and Maj. Robert D. Spencer, HHD 109 HHD 109 Ordnance Battalion (Ammo).

SFC Harry B. Walker competes at an inclement pistol-shooting match.

The Delaware National Guard rifle team, at the national Matches at Camp Perry, Ohio, poses on August 21, 1963. Pictured from left to right are (first row) Lt. Col. George R. Walton, Capt. Robert L. Young, SFC Robert T. Connell; (second row) Capt. Charles R. Painter, S.Sgt. Edward Hadaway III, CWO 2 Harold R. Welch Jr., and MSG Charles E. Wiggins.

The Delaware National Guard pistol team poses at Camp Perry, Ohio, in 1964. As stated on the back of the image, pictured from left to right are Lt. Col. George R. Walton, State HHD; Maj. Michael F. Riley Jr., State HHD; Maj. Russell, U.S. Air Force Dispensary; Maj. Robert D. Spencer, HHD 109 Ord Btn (Ammo); and Capt. Bruce R. Walton, HHD 109 Ord Bn. (Ammo.)

Sgt. Allen G. Russell, Headquarters Battery, 3rd Battalion, 198th, fires his weapon in 1959.

The Delaware National Guard rifle team poses at Camp Perry, Ohio in 1965. As stated on the back of the image, pictured from left to right are (first row) SFC Robert T. Connell of the HHD 109 Ord Bn (Ammo), SPC 5 Terry H. Burchenal of the HHB 2 (AW) Bn, MSG Donald M. Rhoads Jr. of the HHB 1 (AW) Bn, MSG Charles E. Wiggins of the 166 CAM Sq, Sgt. Charles A. Thuet of the HHD 109 Ord Bn (Ammo), and SPC 5 Eugene A. Rodowicz of the 249th Ord Co; (second row) Lt. Col. George R. Walton of the State HHD; S.Sgt. Walter A. Neidig of the Btry D 1 (AW) Bn, CWO 3 Harold R. Welch Jr. of the HHB 2 (AW) Bn, Capt. Robert L. Young of the HHB 3 (AW) BN, Capt. Earle E. Worthington of the HHB 2 (AW) Bn, and SFC George W. Ryder of the Btry C 2 (AW) Bn.

The C Battery, 4th Battalion Field Kitchen sets up its equipment at Delaware Park in May 1960.

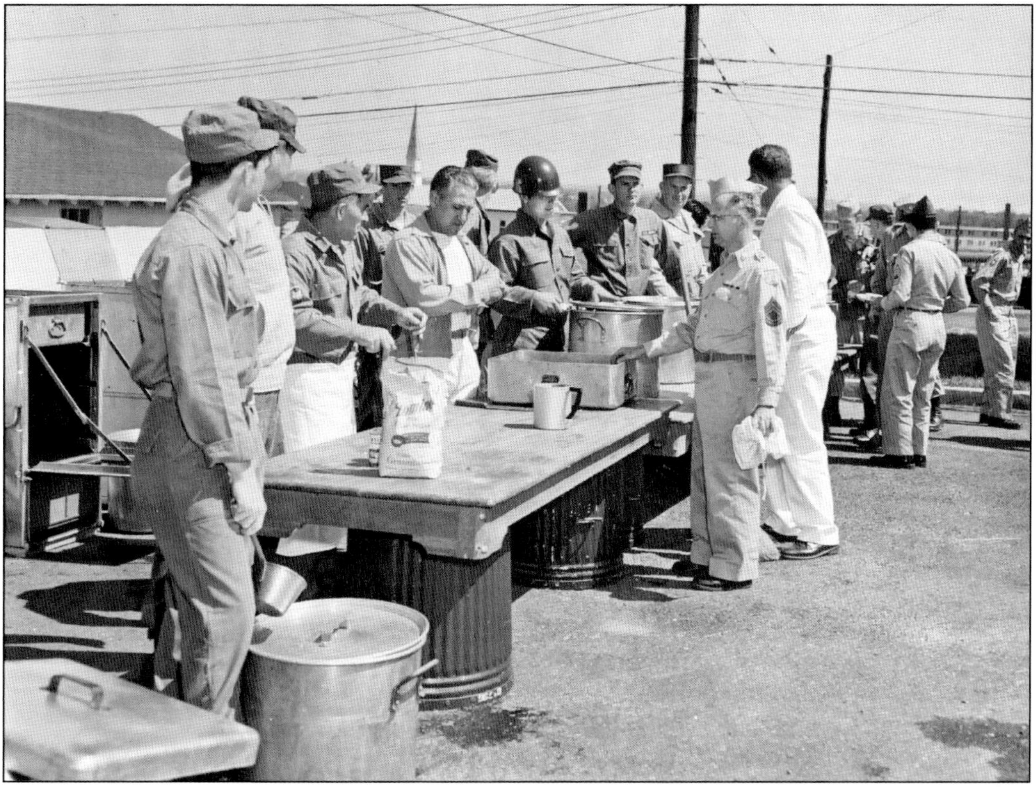

The 736th 4th ADA Battery Mess is depicted at the New Castle Airport during annual field training.

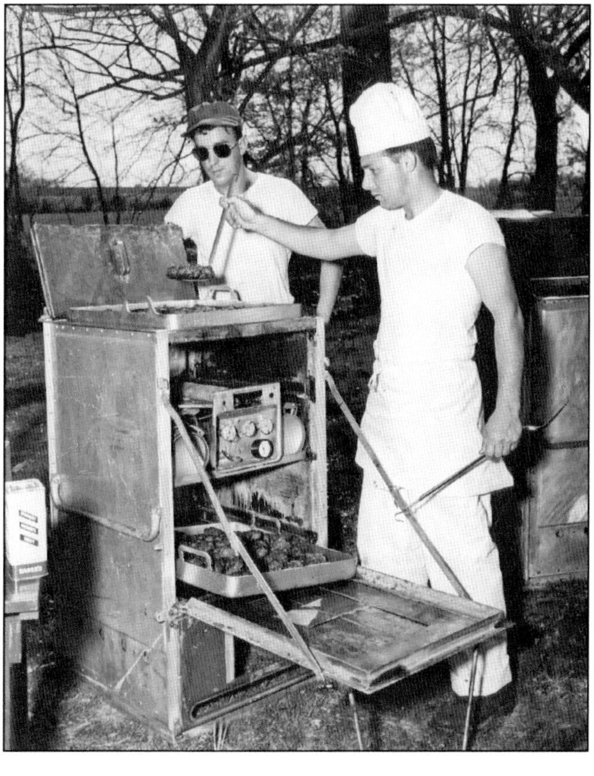

A field kitchen at Delaware Park in May 1960 is manned by SPC 4 James P. Corralin and SPC 5 Lawrence J. Paird of the 4th Battalion, 198th.

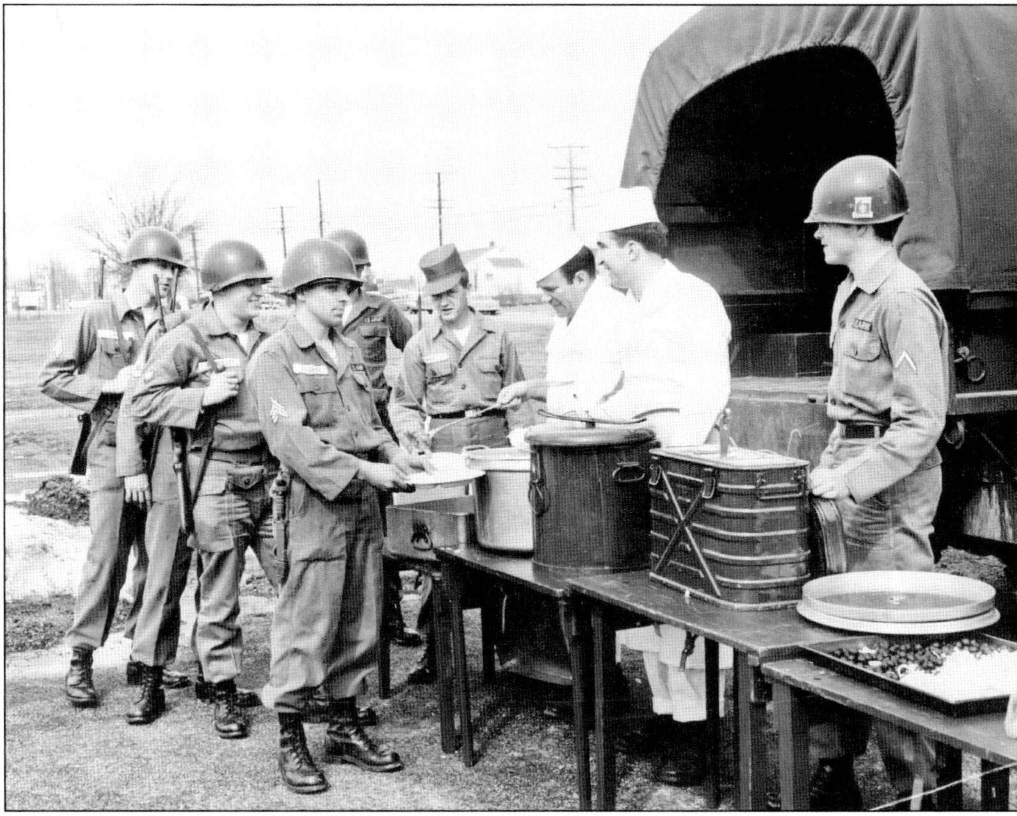

Queuing for chow at a field kitchen "chuck wagon" in Newport are members of B Battery, 1st Battalion, 198th AAA in 1960. Pictured here from left to right are Buck Sergeant Carter; SPC 5 McMullen; Sgt. William Wegman; unidentified; S.Sgt. Eugene Whaley, mess sergeant; SPC 5 Francis Giofre, cook; and PFC George Harrington.

A common summertime sight for travelers and tourists was convoys of soldiers to annual summer camp at the Delaware beach resorts in 1966.

Sgt. William Hayes of D Battery, 4th Battalion, 198th Artillery poses on the steps of the Wilmington Armory with a ceremonial flag holder festooned with Delaware National Guard battle campaign colors starting with New Sweden on August 31, 1655.

Under the warm canvas, a crowded command post guides the 5th Battalion, 198th. Pictured here from left to right are Maj. Harold J. Coulburn, SPC 4 John B. Laine, Maj. Clifford E. Hall (executive officer), and Cpl. Barton T. James in 1959 at Bethany Beach.

Men of A Battery, 193rd Dover, demonstrate their weapon at Bethany Beach in 1953.

The Bethany Beach training site main facility is depicted with the ocean (unseen) to the left in this 1950s photograph.

The South Range at Bethany Beach is crowded with an array of equipment and a Quonset hut.

The South Range tower at Bethany Beach dominates the training skyline.

The D Battery, 1st ADA Battalion (90-mm) gun crew practices loading its gun. MSG Paul Payton is in charge (far right), and the crew, from left to right, includes Sgt. John Holliday, SPC 4 Louis DeBoto, and SPC 3 William Harrison.

PFC Jay P. Moyer of B Battery, 5th Battalion, 198th AAA converses on a field phone during summer camp in 1959.

Guard PFC Thomas M. Hollings of 2nd Battalion, Headquarters Battery guides trucks of the 5th Battalion, Headquarters Battery at summer encampment in 1959.

Men of Battery B, 198th Coast Artillery take aim with their anti-aircraft artillery on the sands of Bethany Beach.

SPC 4 Robert S. Kirkpatrick of 262nd Ordnance Company operates an auxiliary power generator during summer camp in 1959.

Getting ready to put the 90-mm gun in operation are PFC William Cheeseman and Pvt. John Sill of C Battery, 156th ADA Battalion.

Pvt. Milton Canlter of B Battery, 736th ADA Battalion (90-mm gun) demonstrates the operation of the weapon.

An equipment demonstration is depicted during Armed Forces Day in May 1958.

Maj. William A. Smith of Milford's 160th Group of the Delaware Army National Guard plants a simulated atomic demolition kit on the beach at Broadkill. The device was used in a problem staged by the group for the 1st Battalion, 198th Artillery as part of their annual summer training.

The characteristic mushroom cloud of a blast rises hundreds of feet into the air near Georgetown, Delaware, as part of the Delaware National Guard's simulated combat training during annual field training in August of 1960. The cloud is produced by a training device using trinitrotoluene (TNT) and jellied gasoline.

Pvt. Desmond T. Markey, 197th AA, converses on a field telephone at Bethany Beach in the 1950s. (Courtesy Brendan Mackie collection.)

Intelligence operations are conducted at the Bethany Beach range in 1959. In the photograph, from left to right, are MSG Parkes, Colonel Mulrooney, and MSG Lord.

"Milford boys" Capt. Bayard Holleger, battery commander of Headquarters Battery, 160th Group, oversees the paperwork of MSG Herbert C. Jump and SFC Edgar L. Broyles in 1961.

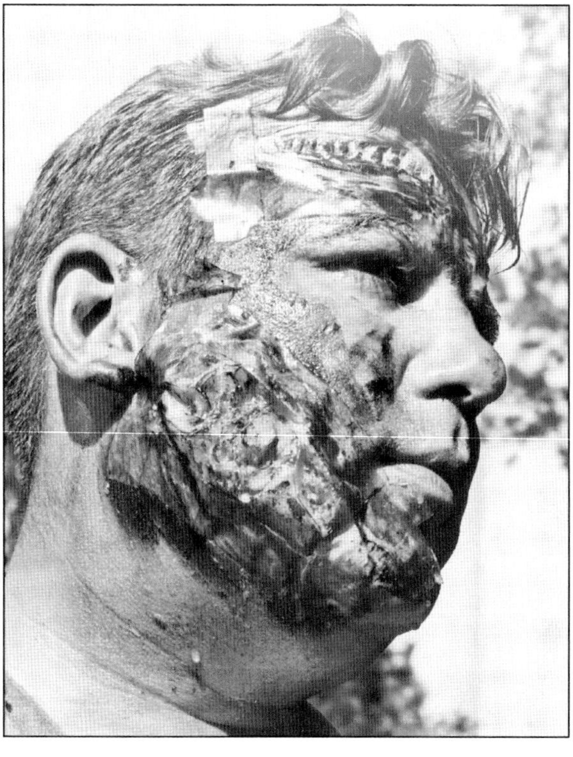

"Accident victim" SFC John Smeyda of the 261st Brigade Headquarters demonstrates "moulage" (simulated) facial injuries during a training exercise in July 1963.

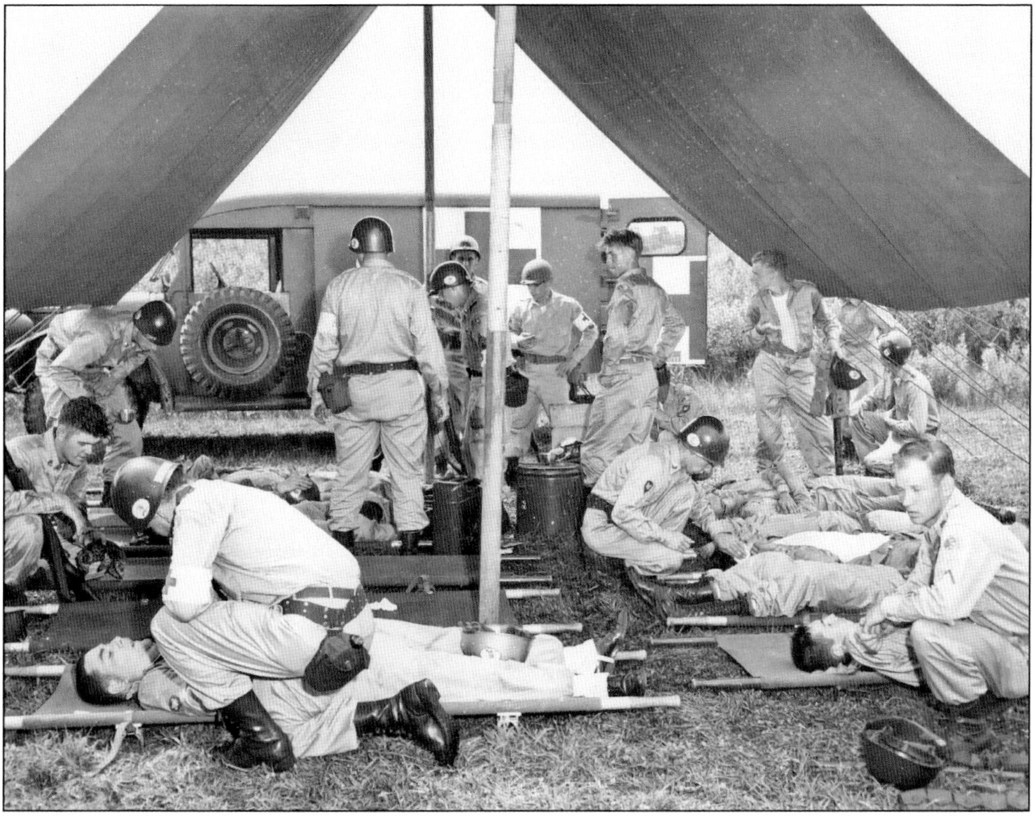

The personnel of the 116th Surgical Hospital conduct a triage exercise in 1966.

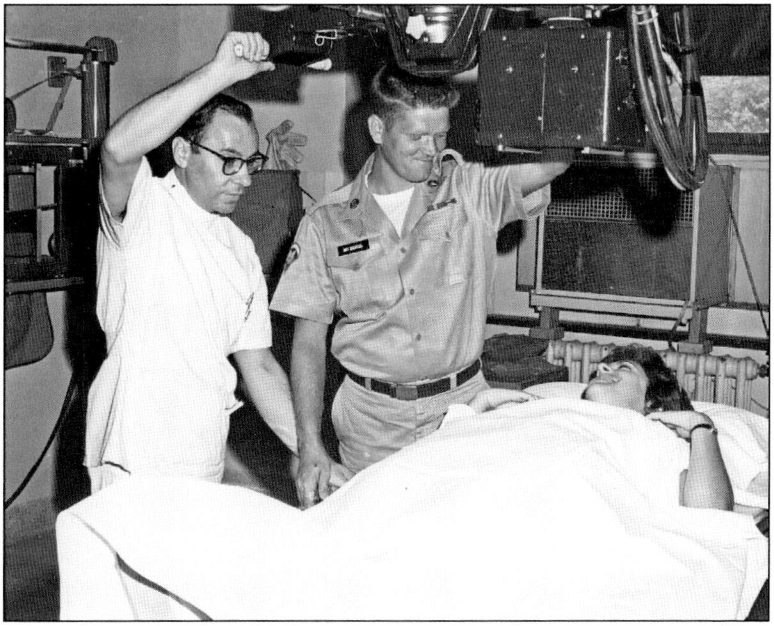

Mike Pastusak, Delaware Hospital x-ray department chief technician, and SPC 5 Theodore McDaniel perform a patient x-ray as training for the 116th Mobile Army Surgical Hospital, otherwise known as MASH, in 1966.

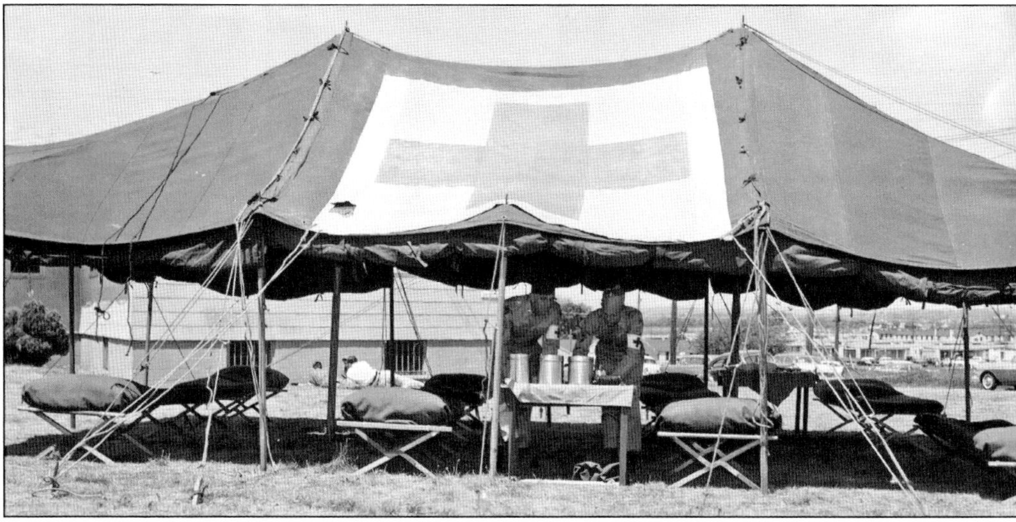

A MASH field tent demonstration is held on Armed Forces Day in May 1959.

The 116th Medical Detachment is depicted on duty during the Berlin Crisis in November 1961 at Fort Campbell Kentucky. SPC 6 Harold White (left) and MSG Anthony Kotch are pictured. Members of the 109th Ordnance Battalion Headquarters Detachment of Middletown served at Aberdeen Proving Ground, Maryland. The 116th MASH was stationed at Fort Campbell, Kentucky, in support of the Airborne Division, and the 1049th Transportation Company went to Fort Meade, Maryland.

SPC 2 Grover Biddle of the 193rd Medical Detachment, Headquarters Battery, 2nd ADA Battalion demonstrates a first-aid procedure.

Lt. Joan Russell of the 116th Mobile Army Surgical Hospital performs training at New Castle Airport in 1966.

The Governor's Ball in 1963 was held in the Wilmington Armory. Note the tropical theme with parrots, umbrellas with garlands, and a parachute suspended from the ceiling.

Miss Battery "B," of 3rd Battalion, 198th, poses on an M-42 Duster with her finery during Muster Day in 1960.

The 109th Ordnance Battalion is welcomed home by Boy Scout Troop No. 94 from active service after the Berlin Crisis in 1962. Lt. Col. Walton accepts the plaque. During the Berlin crisis of 1961, for the first time in its history, the National Guard achieved its objective without combat.

A welcome-home ceremony for all reserve units arriving back from summer training was held at Delaware Park in Stanton on August 18, 1962. Pictured from left to right are Wilmington mayor John Babiarz, Maj. Gen. Joseph J. Scannell, Colonel Seitz, and Delaware governor Caleb Boggs.

Col. Albert Adams pins a decoration upon his son, Sgt. James Adams, in 1964.

Son and father, Lt. Herbert Wardell and Brigadier General Wardell, receive recognition at a decoration ceremony in 1965.

This image depicts the Headquarters 261 Brigade. PFC Lee Eldridge (left), a member of the demonstration team, and SPC 4 Ronald J. Salomon, assistant instructor, conduct an outdoor class in camouflage in October 1960.

A soldier takes a shower in field conditions during the annual field training in 1961.

A soldier performs personal grooming under field conditions in 1961. (Nice haircut too!)

MSG Joe Dugan, also known as "Irish Joe," served five years in World War II and 17 years in the Delaware National Guard with Headquarters Company, 261st Brigade. He is seen here at annual training in 1961. Joe was also a Wilmington Post Office mailman.

A barracks card game for State Headquarters Detachment men is shown, and the men playing include, from left to right, SFC James Oller, MSG Thomas Toy, SPC 5 Francis Toy, and Pvt. Lawrence Sullivan. Sullivan later became a noted lawyer and public defender.

Sgt. William Wegman of B Battery, 1st Battalion enjoys a cup of "Joe," in 1961.

An aggressor (second from the right) is captured by three members of Battery D, First Battalion, 198th Artillery during a tactical problem at Broadkill Beach. Making the capture are, from left to right, PFC Ronald D. Celli, SPC 4 James J. Pullan, and SPC 4 William F. Rees. The aggressor was from the 160th Air Defense Group of the Delaware Guard.

CWO 4 Ed Clinton, also known as "Chief Trip Hammer," gives a wave in 1961.

Delaware Air Guard C-97s await Delaware Army Guard troops for airlift to an exercise in Virginia.

Men of the Headquarters Battery, 4th AW Battalion (SP), 198th Artillery are shown boarding a C-97 at the start of an airlift to Richmond, Virginia, for a field-problem exercise in April 1963.

Maczynski, a strong soldier, hefts a pair of heavy duffel bags onto the back of a "6x6" truck during annual field training at Bethany Beach in 1967.

In March 1962, over 2,000 Delaware Army and Air Guardsmen were called upon for rescue, security, and recovery operations in the devastated coastal areas of Kent and Sussex Counties. In addition, the Dusters were used to get through several severe snowstorms during that time period.

Six

Cold War and Beyond

As the Total Force policy began to engage, the National Guard found itself increasingly asked to do more than stand as a force in reserve. The utility of this initiative came into play during the Gulf War. In November 1990, the 249th Engineer Detachment and the 736th Supply and Service Battalion of the Delaware Army National Guard were placed on alert status and very shortly thereafter placed on active duty to participate in Operation Desert Shield.

The 249th was a 70-person unit consisting of carpenters, electricians, brick masons, plumbers, and pipe fitters whose mission was to provide facilities engineering at fixed installations. Their mission in Saudi Arabia was to maintain a military base camp with the number of personnel reaching 25,000.

The 736th had over 60 personnel who provided services to troops in the field. They distributed supplies and food, controlled critical inventory, and managed logistics for King Khalid Military City.

The Iraq War began on March 20, 2003, with the U.S. and U.K.–led invasion against Saddam Hussein's terror-based regime. Since then, the Delaware National Guard has vigilantly supported Operation Iraqi Freedom. Soldiers and airmen from all across the state answered their country's call once again.

Delaware army and air units and individuals have supported Operation Iraqi Freedom since 2003. The first of these units to arrive in Baghdad was the 249th Engineer Detachment. The 249th was federally mobilized from February 2003 to April 2004. The detachment supported reconstruction efforts throughout the capital city of Baghdad, Iraq. The 249th Engineers completed their mission without casualties, in spite of small-arms fire and rocket and mortar attacks.

The Delaware National Guard is in an almost continuous state of employment serving as an operational force for the U.S. Army. Members have deployed around the world in nation-building exercises, peacekeeping missions, and in support roles for ground combat. They are poised to continue a tradition of service over 350 years long on behalf of the state of Delaware and the United States of America.

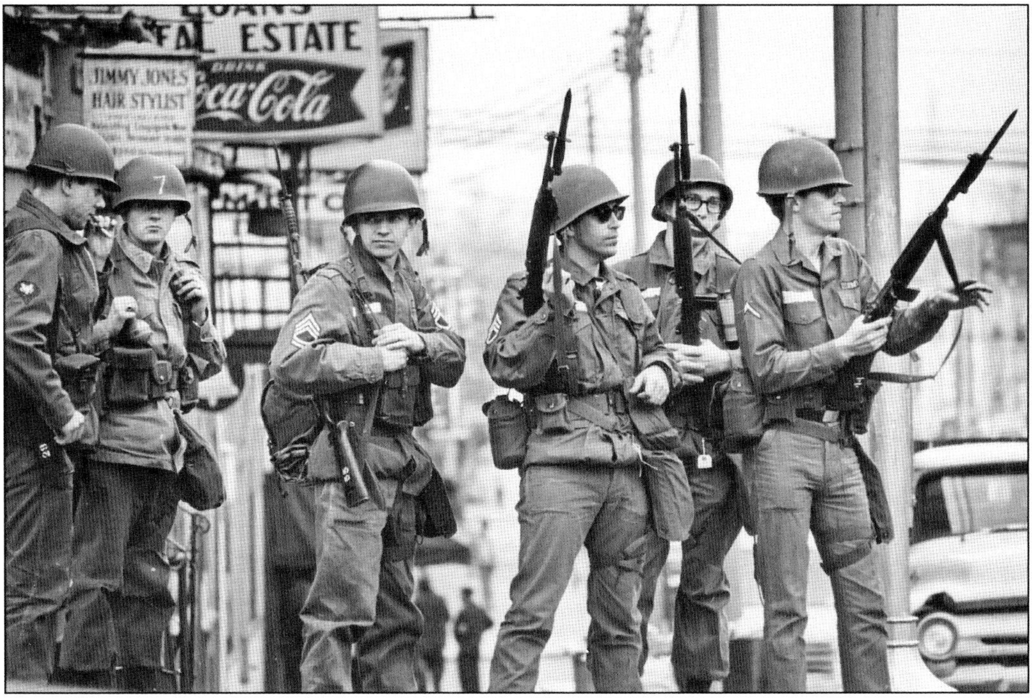

Martin Luther King was assassinated on April 4, 1968. On April 8, civil unrest began in Wilmington, including vandalism, firebombing, and looting. The National Guard was called up for the state emergency.

Approximately 3,500 guardsmen were activated from both the Delaware Army and Air National Guard. They took up posts around the city on April 9, 1968.

Here a curfew is being enforced. Schools, courts, and government offices were closed for the King memorial services. Electrical power was cut off to the west side of town as firebombing continued for a third day.

On Easter Sunday, April 14, 1968, the immediate emergency was declared over. The mayor requested a withdrawal, but the governor refused although demobilization was largely accomplished the next day. Officially the National Guard remained on patrol until the following January when the newly elected governor withdrew them.

Delaware National Guardsmen pay tribute to the late Sen. Robert F. Kennedy as the funeral train passes through Wilmington's Penn Central Station. The military formation joined 5,000 other Delawareans mourning the late senator in 1968.

Lt. Anthony J. Quattro sits for a formal portrait taken in 1970.

Maj. Gen. William Duncan (left) and Brig. Gen. Painter salute for the camera in December 1980.

PFC Andrews pauses to study his manual while on convoy duty.

Captain Emerson, commandant, greets a new candidate to the Delaware National Guard Academy for officer training, offering a pamphlet entitled "Your OCS fact pamphlet" in 1961.

Officer Candidate Greigg receives guidance from three instructors simultaneously in 1968.

This photograph appears to be a faculty inspection for student contraband at the Delaware National Guard Academy Officer's Candidate School in 1966.

Officer candidate student cadets are taught the proper way to march while on all fours.

An officer candidate instructor supervises push-ups among officer candidates in 1966.

An officer candidate tries out his locker for size while being supervised by two instructors in 1966.

Second Lt. Mike O'Neil receives his first salute as a graduating officer and pays an unknown noncommissioned officer the traditional dollar.

Graduating officer candidate 2nd Lt. Nathan Hayward is flanked by his sweetheart and his mother, Rosa McDonald, in 1966.

Bethany Beach South Range radio-controlled aerial targets (RCAT) are depicted launching in 1965. The RCATs are valued at $2,800 and travel at a speed of 220 miles per hour.

Members of the 6th Detachment, 198th Artillery prepare to send an RCAT in flight for target firing by the Delaware Army National Guard's 4th Battalion, 198th Artillery. Pictured, from left to right, are SPC 4 Richard Reed, SPC 5 Del Simpson, and SPC George Baull.

A RCAT (Radioplane OQ-19) of the 6th Detachment is shown here.

The M-42 Duster is a full-tracked, self-propelled, turret-mounted vehicle with dual 40-mm automatic M2A1 Bofors guns augmented by an air-cooled .30-caliber machine gun. This Duster is from C Battery, 3rd Battalion, 198th Artillery.

Dusters are situated in the sand at South Range on Bethany Beach in 1964. The M-42 weapon served with the Delaware National Guard from 1962 to 1970.

M-42 Dusters are depicted here in an echelon formation. Early in 1966, a number of Army Guard enlisted specialists volunteered for six months service as instructors at Fort Bliss, Texas, when the U.S. Army found it lacked men capable of training new personnel about the intricacies of the M-42 Duster. In this select force were seven Delaware units—the five batteries of the 1st Battalion, 198th Artillery and the 116th MASH and 1049th Transportation Company—comprising about one-third of the Delaware Army Guard strength.

An M-42 Duster is being guided by an L-19 spotter plane on the Bethany Range.

The arrival of the first Delaware Guard helicopter is depicted here in 1959. Pictured are Gov. Caleb Boggs (left) and Capt. Dixon Van Landyt.

An ARNG ROTC special program 198th Aviation Company orientation was held in May 1964 in a U-6A Beaver. University of Delaware cadets attached to the state headquarters, from left to right, include Parker, Gavatos, Lenderman, and Craven.

Capt. James R. Sulpizi inspects a U-6A Beaver in August 1960. James was the first state aviation officer for Delaware.

The first drill of the 198th Aviation Company is depicted here with Comdr. Maj. James Sulpizi (far left) in May 1963.

A Delaware Army National Guard Bell UH-1E "Huey" is alighting to secure a cargo.

CWO 2 Blair Messner demonstrates to new pilots and crew chiefs the proper way to secure the patient litter in a UH-1 helicopter in 1988.

A recruiting Jeep is driven on the boardwalk by Dennis Harris at the popular summer resort of Rehoboth, Delaware.

Soldiers rest on a deployment to Germany aboard a North Carolina ANG C-124 for REFORGER, a NATO exercise to "reinforce Germany."

The 101st Public Affairs Detachment poses on a deployment to Honduras during annual training. Pictured among the group are Capt. Ruth Irwin (third from left), 1st Lt. Rita Wiley (sixth from left), and Comdr. Maj. Laura Sievert (seventh from left).

A field exercise was held in September 1980 and included, from left to right, Kenneth Sutton, unidentified, and Capt. Eric Roberson. (Courtesy Eric Roberson collection.)

The remains of CWO 2 Curry are transported home to Dover Air Force Base on September 2, 1985. Curry was the unfortunate victim of an accident during exercise "Bright Star" in Egypt.

Soldiers of the 249th Engineering Company stand in formation prior to deploying to Desert Shield.

Spectators wave to the deploying troops as they convoy for their mobilization station for Operation Desert Shield during the Gulf War.

Consistent with our mission to preserve history on a local level, this book was printed in South Carolina on American-made paper and manufactured entirely in the United States. Products carrying the accredited Forest Stewardship Council (FSC) label are printed on 100 percent FSC-certified paper.

MADE IN THE USA